SUCCESS PHILOSOPHY
STANDING ON THE SHOULDERS
OF SLEEPING GIANTS

iUniverse books may be ordered through booksellers or by contacting:

*iUniverse
1663 Liberty Drive
Bloomington, IN 47403
www.iuniverse.com
1-800-Authors (1-800-288-4677)*

*ISBN: 978-1-5320-4623-0 (sc)
ISBN: 978-1-5320-4624-7 (e)*

Library of Congress Control Number: 2018903812

Print information available on the last page.

iUniverse rev. date: 04/06/2018

CONTENTS

PROLOGUE

"What are you going to do next boy!? You've already done it all!" ROSE MACDONALD

Well, this book answers that question, Grandma Rose.

I dedicate this book to my son Daniel Francis, my daughter Aliyah Dawn, my lovely grandmother Rose Macdonald, my strong grandfather Murray Macdonald, and my ever-loving mother Christina Macdonald. Thank you for guiding, guarding and protecting me until I was strong enough to do so for myself and for others.

I also dedicate this book for the *YOUTH OF TOMORROW AND TODAY.* Make the most of yourselves and we all will win. This is for all those who have no one to pray for them. I hope this information gets into your hands and into your minds and hearts. That is why I'm doing this: so that you know that I am here for you.

I teach all these same things of my own kids. And if you had a strong, rich, successful Dad, then he'd sit here and drill this into your head until your ear fell off. This is to show you that you too have the ability to succeed. I will guide you to do it and convince you that yes, you can do it.

We are truly blessed to have people in the world who are focused on advancement for all. I especially appreciate people like my brother Luke Skaarup, Mel Pervais, Ken Boshcoff and even Terry Fox who literally ran for his and all our lives. J.J. Carrick and the McKellar brothers are some of the sleeping giants that paved the way for the future of our city and our quality of life.

I would particularly like to thank my gorgeous sister Amber Skaarup. She encouraged me to get the show on the road and finish this work pronto.

INTRODUCTION

STANDING UPON THE SHOULDERS OF GIANTS

Standing upon the shoulders of the giants is a habit I learned and adopted years ago after studying Sir Isaac Newton's life. Newton was one of the most influential scientists of all time. When he explained his reasoning about this, a light got turned on inside my head that has never gone out. Isaac made a habit of learning from all the giants that had gone before him. He used their knowledge to further his own success and strengthen his vision. In a child's term it goes like this; monkey see: monkey do! Therefore, I say: find the smartest monkeys and DO WELL!

Giants are just people. They're successful people, past and present, known and unknown to you. They exist is every possible area of expertise. There are mentors waiting to guide you. The idea is, that a giant lifts you up with knowledge and understanding, and once "sitting on their shoulders" you get to see what would otherwise take you a lifetime to figure out on your own. Sitting on their shoulders you may even see things that you would otherwise never have been able to see. Giants can and do help you make the impossible, possible.

WHEN YOU CAN SEE YOUR POTENTIAL, THEN YOU HAVE THE OPPORTUITY TO MAKE IT HAPPEN. The key is to see over YOUR CURRENT HORIZON. Then your vision will resonate at the same frequency that your goal resonates at.

It is my intention to pass on and spread the beneficial habit of standing upon the shoulders of giants. It is a very efficient system of speeding the transmission of knowledge and success through the ages. My number one giant NIKOLA TESLA, said, "The universe is spiritual; we are only half that way. The universe is more moral then us, because we do not know his nature and how to harmonize our lives with it." This book you are reading will help you to harmonize your life with the universe and its laws. One of the giants I have learned a lot from is Neil Degrasse Tyson (whom I lovingly joke or think of as the modern day black Einstein). He speaks of being able to see this principle being used as far back as time itself. Neil Degrasse Tyson is a living giant worthy of standing with the other scientific greats of the ages. Sir Isaac Newton learned that the secret is in geometric arrangement and motion of celestial bodies. Another person I look up to is Bob Proctor, a fellow Canadian from Ontario. Bob is a living wise man, with a true understanding of the mind and all its potential. If you have not heard of him, you are missing out.

Learning from the giants is the most powerful tool I've ever come across and it will help you function at the highest degree possible. I've used this method to brainstorm ideas that have resulted in me creating and owning my own independent construction company in my early 20's and becoming a self-made millionaire before the age of 30. I am after all, just a highly functioning carpenter. Think about what you can do to develop your talents to the fullest. As I am globally publishing this book I just had the most successful month in business of my entire career. I am literally investing some of what I earned IN YOU!! As we make the most of ourselves we all win. Make me proud please and dare to dream big I believe in you and have love for you as well leading me to do this. Write me at Dskaarupconstruction@gmail.com telling me of your victory and I'll be so happy for you 100%.

I live in the land of the Sleeping Giant, an ancient rock formation that looks like a giant man lying down. Across Lake Superior, the world's largest freshwater lake, lays this wonder of Canada. Here in Thunder Bay we take it a bit for granted. It's always there. I am aiming to help guide the youth to go further and faster. That is why I've selected the people featured as guides in this book. As a carpenter it's impossible for me to demonstrate what talents and skills are needed to advance in all the various careers. I've included other people's stories to give a fuller spectrum of talents and success in numerous areas of expertise. I can clearly see that you are not all carpenters, and that's the way it's meant to be. But what we all have in common is the Sleeping Giant. This is what lead me to the title SUCCESS PHILOSHOPHY…. *Standing Upon the Shoulders of Sleeping Giants.*

These inspired stories will get you started and help keep you going. You should aim to find new giants, with talents you admire and want to emulate. Learn and understand their works, then begin building on them at once. With your modern day point of view and technology, maybe you'll achieve some huge breakthrough. Don't be afraid to set your spirit free and let it soar! You need to learn how to harness your all-knowing subconscious: The Universal Mind. You need to be able to visualize your desired outcome. Think like Tesla, Connor McGregor, Bob Proctor. VISUALIZE TO MATERIALIZE.

ALL IS ENERGY, my friend. All. Atoms make up our world and "seem" real, with their electron shells. Atoms make up everything we can touch and all atoms are made up of energy. Energy and matter are interchangeable. Hence $E=MC2$. So are we made of energy they say the energy in the electrons of your body could power a city! You can prove this with a 10,000,000 X view electron microscope. Your subconscious is connected to and influences all atoms.

The ultimate goal is to guide people onto the right path sooner in life by finding their Dharma. We have all heard of Karma, and have become familiar with this concept of the rebalancing of forces. Dharma is your life's purpose. It is your direction. The sooner a person is able to find their way, their dharma, then their development can be greatly enhanced by standing upon the shoulders of giants.

A tree can grow to 379 feet. But understand that if that tree doesn't get enough water or light, it's maximum potential never occurs. The largest living thing on earth is in fact a tree called General Sherman. General Sherman sure did reach its potential and lived 2500 years enjoying ideal conditions. Standing upon the shoulders of giants is a way of creating your own ideal conditions to flourish under. Understand what nourishes you and helps progressively develop your talents. I am now working with Bob Proctor and Sandy Gallagher as a certified consultant. You may remember Bob Proctor from the book The Secret. It sold to the tune of 20-30 million copies and more importantly introduced me to Bob and his genius mindset over a decade ago. You can now hire me in real life as your success coach. Do so and I'll guide you to achieve and goals you want and to become a self-made millionaire if you desire. Email me at Dskaarupconstruction@gmail.com and we'll win together.

TERRY FOX

TRYING, MAKES A DREAM POSSIBLE.

Terry Fox was born in Winnipeg on July 28, 1958 and is arguably one of Canada's most famous athletes. He is also one of the bravest Canadians to date. Terry literally took a road less travelled.

When his life was put in jeopardy with the diagnosis of cancer and the subsequent amputation of his leg just below the hip, Terry became one of the most selfless Canadians in history. Terry became focused on how he could help everyone else. In the battle of his life he clearly saw the bigger picture that most of us cannot see. We are all in this together and we are all connected on many levels. And sometimes helping the whole is far greater then helping the self.

Terry's achievements are nothing short of extraordinary. He was the youngest person in Canada ever to be named a companion of the Order of Canada. He envisioned and created THE MARATHON OF HOPE, now the largest and most successful one-day cancer research fundraiser in the world!! People from around the world, in excess of 60 countries participate in the MARATHON OF HOPE and have raised over $650,000,000.00 in his name, and still counting. Terry felt he owed his life to medical advancement and this drove him to do something about it. It broke Terry's heart to see people fighting for their lives against cancer, first losing their smiles and eventually their lives. Terry felt that he had been cured. Just a few years before, there had been only a 15 percent survival rate for his type of cancer. Thanks to medical advances the survival rate had improved to a 50 percent. Most of these breakthroughs had been made possible through fund raising. This may well have been what planted the seed in his mine that eventually grew into the MARATHON OF HOPE.

Terry was not one to lay around deciding what to do about it. He knew what he was thinking of was going to be hazardous and may even cost him his life. But to Terry all the risks were worth it. This spirit of bravery and selflessness, in the face of a seemingly insurmountable foe, made Canada instantly fall in love with Terry. The emotional connection Terry made Canadians feel was so strong that people felt it deep down. They knew he was offering everything he had to try and help others. He had so much skin in the game. His support grew nationwide. Whether rich or poor, old or young, athletic or not: Terry made people feel that if he could still strive under such harsh adverse conditions, that maybe they should try to do something too. The plan of every Canadian donating $1.00 was nothing compared to the pain Terry was willing to absorb. Terry found after 20 minutes of intense pain, he would have made it through the worst of it and that he could keep going on with less pain. Terry gave his blood, sweat and tears for us. I hold a special place in my heart for Terry. He gives me strength when I am feeling down and feel that my life is difficult. The contrast reminds me that I'm very blessed and that my obstacles are temporary at best and certainly not life threatening. I've included Terry in this book out of my huge respect for him. Our ideas live longer than we do! Terry's MARATHON OF HOPE is an idea that has lives on in the minds of millions with more and more still learning about it. Now that is a big impact.

Here are a few quotes from Terry so you can get a feel for what he was like.

"Everybody seems to have given up the hope of trying. I haven't. It isn't easy, and it's not supposed to be, but I'm accomplishing something. How many people give up a lot to do something good? I'm sure we would have found a cure for cancer years ago if we had really tried."

"I just wish people would realize that anything is possible if you try; DREAMS ARE MADE POSSIBLE IF YOU TRY."

"Even if I do not finish, we need others to continue. It has got to keep going even without me."

"When I started this run, I said, if we all give one dollar, we'd have $22 million for cancer research, and I don't care man, there is no reason that that isn't possible. No reason."

You see his unshakeable belief my friends? Many people told Terry many reasons why it was not possible. $650,000,000 million dollars later, they can eat a crow sandwich. He did TRY AND IT WAS MADE POSSIBLE. Who knows, Terry may have died anyways and instinctively he knew, it was either do this with his life or do nothing!

After 143 days and 5,373 km, just outside of Thunder Bay, Terry's part of the marathon ended. After running half way across Canada on one leg, his cancer came back and took his life, but thankfully not before his MARATHON OF HOPE was established and given to the world. There stands an amazing memorial in his honor just outside of Thunder Bay. Terry's statue majestically overlooks Lake Superior and the Sleeping Giant. I take my family to this monument every so often and it is beautiful. Terry was loved and honored by so many. In his honor dozens of schools, many roads, building, monuments and even a mountain range now carry his name forward. He may not have lived a long life, but his name will never die. Look him up and see many more of Terry's extraordinary achievements. The list is long and impressive. He will also live on in this book as a result of his ideas, mental intensity and respect!

TRYING MAKES IT POSSIBLE

On a quantum level let us look at the one thing Terry wanted us to know: that TRYING MAKES IT POSSIBLE. Trying, with a focused intention combined with energetic action and commitment, make it possible to achieve whatever goal you set.

Quantum physicists have discovered some very spooky things on the subatomic level. Using countless advances in modern science and technology, they have discovered that particles do not choose a charge, positive or negative, until someone checks on them! The act and intention of checking makes the particle choose a charge and shows what it is. So what does that mean for us? Well, it proves that our minds, our thoughts, our intentions can and do cause changes in the material world around us. Even spookier than that, some particles are on a quantum level entangled across space and when one particle choose to become positive, the other entangled particle instantaneously becomes negative. There is FAR more going on in the universe than we can see and understand, FAR MORE. We just can't see or understand it YET. It is widely known that the majority of the universe is a substance called dark matter. We haven't quite yet grasped what dark matter is. We can just tell that it is there. In the same way, we all largely operate with a "the earth is flat" mentality when it comes to regarding some of the unseen actions of the universe. "If I can't see it or touch it, then it's fake." This only closes our minds to possibilities. If you think the earth is flat, you will close your mind to all other possibilities and you won't ever bother to TRY to open your eyes.

Terry was energetic and brave, so he did try. THANK YOU TERRY! And further, he kept on trying no matter what. He made the impossible, possible. It only became reality once Terry took the steps necessary to make it happen.

You can create your own future and destiny this way. The actions you take and the moves you make will open up new futures for you. You first have to pick up some weights and lift them if you want the future possibility of becoming Ontario's Strongest Man. When Terry's own mum didn't believe in what he was doing, Terry kept on trying even though he was deeply hurt. He had thought that she'd be first in line to believe in his plan and his intentions. A lot of people said a lot of things against Terry's plan, but Terry bravely went on and tried his best no matter what. He tried so much that people's hearts felt for him and they felt compelled to help make his dream come true. I have a strong feeling compelling me to help guide those that need it, and are willing to open their eyes to any sort of future they can imagine.

The universe is all connected you see. Your body is not separate from it. You are a part of the giant particle sea of energy. We're an energy form wearing a meat suit. We are all made up of atoms, just like everything else in the world. Atoms are 99% hollow space with an electron shell orbiting them (electricity). So on a quantum level, we are energy and electrical and particles put together in an organized state and are intrinsically connected to all others. E=MC2 tells us basically that energy and mass are interchangeable. C is the speed of light. So Energy = Mass x (speed of light x speed of light) shows the energy you get by turning matter into energy. The universe can and does turn energy into matter and vice versa non-stop. The stars in fact have created all the materials we need for our journey. Adding or removing electrons from the shell of an atom creates all the elements used for creation of this material plane. The more you learn about fundamental particles the more you realize that spooky stuff CAN AND DOES happen all the time.

Consider the existence of a universal mind that is intrinsically entangled with the material world of particles. The basic universal laws like gravity had to come from somewhere. Einstein said that as a kid he could see this spooky invisible force in action when he observed what a magnet could do. Two magnets can pull or push at each other with an invisible force that you can feel but not see. The science bug bit Albert so hard that he always loved thinking about the invisible forces at play in our world. Einstein says that the invisible force that you can't see but can feel in a magnet was all the proof he needed to know that even an unseen force can be real. E=MC2 creates much of our energy. Many things work even though it seems as though they shouldn't. A finger-tip size of uranium can produce the same amount of electrical power as 5000 barrels of oil. Mankind is even learning to "play god" a bit by adding electrons and creating new elements not found in the universe.

If checking makes a particle take on a charge, then just maybe by trying, fundamental particles can be affected. Wise men of all ages have known the supreme POWER OF INTENTIONS. Believing is the first step to creating form from the formless. Trying is your focused intention combined with energetic effort. The more I learn, the more I'm starting to think that they are bang on. We are beginning to understand the previously misunderstood. Now consider the existence of a universal mind that is intrinsically entangled with our own thoughts.

COSMIC CONSCIOUSNESS, THE UNIVERSAL MIND

Ok, yeah, yeah, I know we are maybe venturing too deep here, but understanding that what I'm laying down here can positively affect your life, so I'm writing it anyways.

Become aware now, if you aren't already, that you are a spiritual being with a mind (conscious and subconscious) and a body (made up of atoms and energy, the same as everything else in the universe). There IS a universal mind that seems to be a repository for all of mankind's thoughts and deeds, and lucky for us our subconscious mind is connected to it. We are all energy. Everything is energy. What we think of as solid, say a table, is made up of atoms. Atoms can now be seen with a 10,000,000 X electron microscope. Atoms gain the hardness that we touch or even stub our toe on, from the electron shell surrounding each atom. Electrons orbit the proton at 5 million miles an hour! These same electrons run through the wires in your homes and schools as electricity. Our minds are able to communicate with every atom in the universe. Thoughts are electrical waves on specific frequencies. By imaging the picture of your desired outcome, you set your mind and it passes this thought energy out to the universe where it begins to take form. The universe responds to your images and thought. Your imagination has the power to order and construct atoms. Tesla invented the remote control in his imagination, just like all inventions are first created in the mind. How many remote controls are there in existence in our material world today? How many atoms were used to materialize these remote controls? A sheet of paper is

500,000 atoms thick. Never underestimate the power of your mind, your imagination, and your intent.

So do we all agree: that if Terry didn't try, it would have remained impossible, and would never have materialized. He tried to raise $1.00 from every Canadian and far surpassed his goal, reaching over $650,000,000.00 for cancer research in his name.

Now I would like to introduce some of the giants form our area that were able to create form from the formless. I hope we can all learn something from them. Many people think that the only way to succeed in life is to have someone, hopefully their parents, hand it all to you on a silver platter. Well let me tell you, most of these giants succeeded through their own vision and their own hard work. Many were born with very little and literally pulled themselves up by their bootstraps.

THE MCKELLAR BROTHERS

Father: Duncan McKellar
Mother: Margaret Brodie (they immigrated from Scotland)

Brothers: John, Peter, Donald and Archibald.

These four brothers were as lucky as a four-leaf clover. I like to think of LUCK as Labor Under Correct Knowledge. That being the case, the McKellar brothers sure had the correct knowledge indeed. In the late 1800's, the bothers owned the deed to much of down-town Fort William's most valuable land. These Ultra ambitious characters made a success of whatever they set their hands, hearts and minds to. They created a massive subdivision, which led to the creation of Fort William (now Thunder Bay). The city of Thunder Bay owes its existence, in part, to these pioneering men.

The McKellar's were true visionaries in every sense of the word. They tried. They worked hard. They were able to create things of value and substance that had long lasting impact. Being brave enough to start building a town, they must have had guts.

Their projects and investments were very diverse and included copper mines, gold mines and silver mines. They created subdivisions; went into politics and contributed philanthropy to many. Many of the streets of Thunder Bay are still named after them. You can still see pictures of Peter and John McKellar, big beards and all, on a Shopper's Drug Mart near the old McKellar Hospital on Arthur St.

What I see as their greatest accomplishment was getting CP rail to locate in our area. We need good jobs more than anything else. Many people miss the fact that real estate is only valuable if there are jobs nearby. I can build you a million-dollar mansion but if you decide to locate in Red Rock, it may be worth only $300,000. I can tell you that the McKellar brothers had a firm grasp on this concept and it played heavily into the strategy they employed. They purchased undeveloped land at one dollar an acre. They subdivided the land, developed it, brought in the railway, which provided jobs for many and then sold their developments at a major profit. They became very wealthy while providing housing and long-term jobs for many. My father Dale Skaarup fed us children with money he earned while working at that CP Rail facility. One of the special memories I have that was influenced by all this, is driving a train with my Dad at ten years of age and feeling like a king. The jobs that the McKellar's brought were most importantly of a long lasting nature, not an easy feat. Thousands of residents in Thunder Bay live and eat atop of the McKellar's early efforts.

ACCOMPLISHMENTS OF THE MCKELLAR BROTHERS:

1860 - McKellar brothers move to Thunder Bay dreaming of success in mining.

1866 - McKellar family owns 6,000 acres in mineral land holdings. The brothers develop many mines, which they later sell for enormous profits.

1868 - John builds his house, settles down and lives here for the rest of his life.

1874 - Peter publishes and edits the town's first newspaper: The Perambulator.

1875 - The McKellar brothers buy the family farm: 173 acres for $173.00.

1875 - They subdivide part of the farm and create 143 building lots.

1880 - John negotiates the sale of part of the family farm to CP Rail. The development of the railway drove his and everyone else's property values way up. This also created jobs of a long lasting nature and gelled the formation of the city. John's business wits provided prosperity and health for a land mass roughly the size of France. Thunder Bay now has a $375,000,000.00 hospital that serves as a medical hub for all of Northwestern Ontario.

1887 - 1889 - The McKellar brother subdivide the farm again, creating 400 more building lots.

1889 - Peter donates the land for St. Andre's Presbyterian Church.

1892 - John becomes mayor of Fort William (Thunder Bay) and holds the position for six years.

1900 - John passes away.

1902 - John's sister, Mary lays the cornerstone for the John McKellar Memorial Hospital on land donated by the McKellar family.

1907 - The McKellar brothers sell 36 acres of the family farm to J.J. Carrick. They had paid 36 dollars for the land in 1875 and 32 years later sold it to Carrick for $155,000.00.

2016 - Peter and John McKellar can still be seen in pictures on Shopper's Drug Mart on Arthur St. This was built on land they had donated for McKellar hospital.

Their photos let us know that these men were here, they were smart and did many things to provide us all with the city of Thunder Bay where I live today.

OBSERVATIONS AND LESSONS OF THE MCKELLAR BROTHERS:

- Work hard on large projects that can take years to complete.

- Buy low and sell extra high. Their farm land became 4,305 times more valuable as development and job growth came to Thunder Bay.

- Real estate values can rise rapidly if large employers can be attracted to an area. All mayors have a duty to their citizens to attract companies that can provide jobs.

- If you are able to create great wealth in your lifetime, donate some of your profits to help advance everyone. The Mckellar's donated land to churches, hospitals and parks.

- As you mature go into politics and use your talents to provide advances for us all. Many of your efforts will have a wider influence than you could have imagined.

J.J. CARRICK

John J. Carrick was born in 1873 in Indiana, USA.

He grew up in Ontario, Canada.

J.J. Carrick lived a very interesting life to say the least. Several local legends involve this man and he has been called: One of the most interesting and intriguing people to ever reside in the Lakehead (Thunder Bay).

Carrick worked for John D. Rockefeller (one of the world's richest men) in his early life, selling oil. As an entrepreneur Carrick was greatly influenced by him. It's my personal view that when Carrick came into contact with Rockefeller's level of wealth and success he got bit by the wealth bug so hard, he never got over it.

Carrick became "on fire" with success and momentum and became a very talented salesman. He moved to Thunder Bay to capitalize on the boom he could see coming. He felt "If he can do that then so can I". To others he must have seemed a man possessed. Carrick came to town like a lightning bolt, full of energy and enthusiasm. He managed to partner with some of the biggest names in Thunder Bay on numerous projects.

Many people know of Carrick St. in Thunder Bay, but few know of the ambition it took to be honored with a street named after you. He didn't just slip on a banana peel and it all somehow accidentally fell in his lap. Carrick was brave enough, and some would even call him crazy enough, to dare and build a city.

More than anything, Carrick knew how to motivate people. He was also on hell of a storyteller: like how he won the Prince Arthur Hotel in a poker game. Carrick's creative force influenced many, many people's lives. Someone, somewhere will read this and come to realize that their home and subdivision is in fact, one built by J.J. Carrick. Furthermore, my own sister Amber and niece's Skyla and Bella's home is built atop one of J. J's idea's! In Thunder Bay he helped create more than a dozen subdivisions. Some examples are Victoria Park, Brent Park and Mayday Park (his most successful subdivision that was named after his wife May Day). He also helped create subdivisions in other cities. There is a community in Manitoba name Carrick, after him. Carrick lived a long and prosperous life, well into his 90's.

Your ideas have a life far longer than you. This is something worth pondering.

CARRICK'S ACCOMPLISHMENTS:

1897 - Carrick graduates from university in Toronto. He becomes a leading oil salesman for John D Rockefeller. (The worlds all time richest man inflation corrected!!)

1903 – Carrick moves to Port Arthur, now Thunder Bay. A possible real estate boom attracted him. He begins buying and selling real estate at a shocking rate.

1902 -1910 - With the participation of investors, Carrick creates over a dozen major subdivisions in Thunder Bay: including Victoria Park, Brent Park and Mayday Park. Ever the salesman and promoter, he gave away free building lots to those who accurately predicted that outcome of elections.

1906 – Carrick creates and launches his own newspaper: The Port Arthur Daily News

1907 – Carrick buys 36 acres of the McKellar family farm for a whopping $155,000.00 (around 4 million CAD in modern value). By the age of 34 Carrick has become a self-made millionaire.

1908 – Carrick becomes Mayor of Port Arthur. He wins the election in true J.J. style, never afraid to shine bright.

1908 – the legend of the Prince Arthur Hotel has it that Carrick won the right to develop the hotel in a poker game with Sir William Mackenzie (president of the CN rail line). Carrick must have been amazed to see CN make good on the bet. They paid $850,000.00 to have him build the hotel. The city provided the lot, overlooking Lake Superior and the Sleeping Giant. The hotel was an important stop along the rail line that eventually linked together all of Canada. Royalty have stayed in its spectacular suites. The Prince Arthur Hotel is also the first place in Canada to sell the Remembrance Day poppies. Carrick ability to dream big had a wide influence on a great deal of people and even on the history of Canada.

1910 – During Carrick's political campaigns Carrick was ultra-conspicuous. He did everything in his power to stand out like a neon sign in the dark. As my mentor Bob Proctor would say he stood out like a giraffe in a heard of field mice! His 1910 campaign is a prime example. You can tell from his actions that he believed that "no publicity is bad publicity." Carrick travelled with a "picture machine", an accompanying pianist, a cartoonist, and an impressive baritone call Mr. Foster and a three-man vaudeville act called the Vynos. By this point in his life Carrick had found his stride. With the pedal to the metal, he knew what he wanted, how to get there and most importantly, how to just do it. He imagined the outcome he wanted and had unwavering faith in his abilities to do it.

1910 – Carrick sets up offices in Port Arthur, Fort William, Toronto, Winnipeg and Montreal. He then creates his own mortgage finance company called The Red Path Estate. I love this because when I was 13 my father Dale Skaarup as a CP rail executive had offices in Calgary, Winnipeg and Minneapolis which used to make my head spin.

1911 – 1917 – Carrick serves a MP in the federal government.

OBSERVATIONS AND LESSONS OF J.J. CARRICK:

- If you never try, you'll never win. Try lots to win lots, because you can never win them all.

- His Dharma appears to be a mix of citybuilder, salesman and politician.

- Opportunities multiply as they are seized.

- Start your own business. Even start multiple businesses.

- Live life doing big deals, with big people.

- If you want to increase the speed of your progress, sell fast, sell lots.

- Go into politics, if it suits you, and use your wits to bring jobs, investment and valuable growth to your city.

MEL PERVAIS

Mel Pervais is an ultra-successful Native American entrepreneur and executive and one of my good friends and mentors. He has taught me so much about being a business executive! The Los Angeles Times has rated Mel as one of the world's wealthiest natives. See his Wikipedia page to be mind blown! Mel grew up on Fort William First Nation near Squaw Bay. Mel's story is nothing short of miraculous. I am truly blessed to have been taught by Mel and feel obligated to share some of his wisdom with you the reader.

Mel is a firm believer in "moving where the work IS" and "never settling". When he started his apprenticeship in electrical instrumentation even he had no idea as to how far it would take him. He rose to the top with a can do attitude. "my apprenticeship turned me into a man. I worked for 20 years for different employers, in copper mines, chemical plants and for contracting and engineering companies."

Legends are built not born I say. Mel's legend began growing on a solid foundation of understanding, hard work and 20 years of real life experience. He was now a force to be reckoned with. Being a visionary he could see how to grow a new revenue stream into the millions and did just that. Feeling undervalued and appreciated he made the big decision to start his own business. He had such a good attitude that when working at nuclear plants he was routinely told that if he should ever start his own business that they would hire him in a heartbeat. Upon deciding to do just that his life and success skyrocketed! That decision sent a tsunami of success his way.

Now a CEO and president of his own business he really hit his stride. Bringing his great attitude and charisma into the nuclear power plants he was able to land enough contracts to hire 100's of engineers and see yearly sales that would rival today's top rock stars……. From an apprenticeship at that. His humble beginnings had turned to unbelievable success. He had 3 leer jets 100's of employees and more cash flow than you could shake a stick at, again see his Wikipedia page for more on this. He would even say to the bosses at power plants "I'll have some of my guys flown in here on my leer jet in a few hours to start immediately if you hire us".

Some of his business motto's he used to make things work were

1. Always hire the best personnel for the job
2. Never compromise performance for political reasons
3. Earn the job after acquisition.

4. Never settle for second place.
5. With cost plus you don't need lots of capital you just bill as you go.

After 10 years as an entrepreneur and achieving success beyond his wildest dreams Mel than made the big decision to sell his business to the employee's and live the good life. He had been working 18 hour days to pull this off and decided not to work himself into an early grave. I have noticed with great success also comes great sacrifice of one form or another so beware of the risks you face my friends! At the height of his business success he had 3 leer jets, 100's of employee's, built and owned 2 20 000 ft./2 office buildings and owned 17 different homes during his adventures. He was even hand selected by Ronald Regan to advise him on a task force. Mel jokes that Ronald said " ya know if you call me Ronnie one more time I'm gonna start calling you Melvin from now on".

Upon retirement he really did start enjoying the good life travelling and spending time with his family and friends now that the 18-hour work days were a thing of the past. He bought a 2500-acre ranch Montana where he even built a subdivision and more with his son Brian's help on the big dozer. Many moons passed before our paths did and I am forever great full they did as Mel has been a great friend and mentor to me. He is truly one of my Giants . I think he liked the questions I asked him as it takes one to know one and was always very helping and friendly to teach me. My vision as a CEO has definitely increased after being lifted up on his shoulder so to speak.

KEN BOSHCOFF

FUTURE MAYOR AND MP BORN IN WAASTFORT

'If, as Canadians, we ever had to list our top five blessings then surely among them is the fact that many of us, more that most of humanity before us, grew up in a safe, friendly and clean neighborhood.

...I didn't even know until I was elected mayor of Thunder Bay, that these values were what much of the world was aspiring to. To be raised without fear of starvation, persecution, injustice, intolerance and to have miraculous words like "opportunity, freedom, security, health and prosperity", guide their massive commitment to see their children have a way better life than the ones in which they themselves grew up in.

When values such as these are instilled in youthful thinking, they will later mature into laws and policies enacted by their future selves. Knowing that parents of EVERY ethnic, cultural and religious background all want the SAME things for their kids, helps clarify one's vision. Then it becomes obvious that racism is based on ignorance'.

Where to begin telling the tale of my friend Ken. If ever I have met a giver or a go giver as Bob Proctor likes to say it's Ken. He has sat on more boards than a carpenter. I credit him with teaching me about area's I'm weak in. Unfortunately, his father Tom passed away when he was young. This left a strong impression on him that he would later use as a backbone in politics by being a supporter of labor rights and worker's protections. After watching his mother fight hard to provide for his family as a single mother he wanted to help others. "her hands were as red as blood and she was totally exhausted. She made me look at her hands and made me promise that I would never put gum under my desk. She had spent 15 hours scraping gum from the bottom of desks at school. To this day I never leave any place untidy, whether it's a hotel room or a fishing camp. I know someone like my mother will have to clean up after me and I just can't bear the thought of some poor widow having to work extra hard because I was to selfish".

Luckily he had some male role models. His uncle Frank instilled in him a passion for collecting coins and stamps to this day he credits it with helping him to understand many of the ethnic conflicts today. And his brother Fast Eddy ran Thunder Bays most successful insurance brokerage. He became a president at Westgate student council (found his dharma young). Than was part of the 1960's hippy era at LU even starting a chapter of Greenpeace.

Fate strikes again "my career as a planner ended after four years when my friends and family got me elected as a ward councilor for the Northwood area.... this was a life lesson that has stayed with me ever since. Good people can lose elections."

Ken has accomplished more than I can write in this book with his great attitude even being my favorite Mayor to ever serve in Thunder Bay and being and MP. Anyone suited for politics I advise you to learn from Ken as he is as sharp and humble as they come.

DAN SKAARUP

BILLY THE KID WITH A NAIL GUN BORN AKA THE DANIMAL

I was born on May 7th, 1981 at McKellar Hospital (see how influential the Mckellar brothers were) in Thunder Bay Ontario, Canada. I grew up with my older and always much larger brother, Luke, and with my younger, beautiful sister, Amber. There being only a year and a half between us, we went through everything together and I wouldn't have had it any other way. We grew up in a house built by our parents using old school methods, as the hydro hadn't been hooked up yet. Being a carpenter and homebuilder myself, I can greatly admire this accomplishment.

I grew up on 5 acres (given to my mother) of my grandpa Murray's 400-acre farm in O'Connor Township, just outside of Thunder Bay. Murray was tough and set a great example for Luke and I and our cousin Dave. He showed us what it takes to be a man. There is a picture my grandma

Rose took of him doing a handstand on the chimney of the family camp at Loon Lake. (Now I know where I get my daring spirit from, and my alias as a kid: Dangerous Dan McGroo).

In the early 1940's my grandpa was the strongest light heavy weight in town. He held this title for two years. After having lifted weights for several decades and then becoming a farmer later in life, he was like Stone Cold Steve Austin, but just a tad nicer. If I remember correctly he had a razor strap, a 3-inch-wide thick piece of leather used for sharpening razors, mounted on plaque on the wall. This was to meant to inspire fear into us kids and remind us of what we had coming if you decided to be really bad. Murray could throw 40 to 60-pound hay bales all day long and he'd get you to do it with him. Our pay was Kool-Aid and being taken for a swim down at the Whitefish River if you were lucky.

We just took all this hard work as normal life. You wake up, play or work, do whatever needs doing. No matter how hard it was, we learned to just put our heads down and get it done. Being rather small but exceedingly strong, I was forged into titanium. At Churchill High School in grade nine, I weighed 130 pounds and I could bench press 300 plus pounds. This beat much of the football team, which included many older than myself.

Even my grandpa's nickname was tough, MAC. At 89 years old he was still there. Being an accountant too, he was one of my sharpest business advisors. He always wanted the best for me. He was employed and self-employed as an accountant and farmer for 55 consecutive years. He passed away while I'm writing this and it really made me realize how important that it is that we all have good role models.

My grandmother Rose, on the other hand, was his polar opposite: the yin to his yang. Everywhere he was rough and tough, she was kind and gentle. She is a little lady with a heart of gold and comes with some big ancestors. She moved here from Shetland, Scotland and comes from a long line of teachers. Rose's mother's maiden name was Helen Wallace. Her ancestor was Alexander William Wallace. He must have been a very clever man as he was the private tutor to the sons of the King of Scotland, Robert the Bruce. She and my ancestors trace back to Sir William Wallace's brother and father, Sir Malcom Wallace.... now I know why I'm so brave and tough! For hundreds of years my family has honored the name of William Wallace. They would alternate names like William Alexander Wallace and Alexander William Wallace for generations. You might remember him from the movie *BRAVEHEART*. If you haven't seen it, I urge you to watch it.

And so the saga continues. I worked on the farm since I could walk and started splitting and hauling wood when I was around 7 years old. My grandfather Murray loved to tell me the story of what a brave Wildman I was at 3 years old I chased a wolf with a hatchet that was after his cow's I ran after it fearlessly as he grinned and laughed. Growing up in the country, we had a large area of about 50 km as our turf. My best friend Birch's house was a 10 km bike trip away, a round trip of 20 km. Usually I wouldn't even dare bike there unless I knew it was for a sleepover. We grew up strong, smart, tough and fast. Given free time, we would build tree houses and then throw pretend hand grenades at each other.

We grew up watching Barry Third of TBT News. The funny thing was that until I was about 10, I thought his name was Barry the Third. We listened to Mark Tannehill on the Rock 94... I still listen to Rock 94 now it's Cale and Dee. We loved watching the WWE, while consuming a steady diet of Stallone, the Dukes of Hazard, He Man and lots of Arnold movies. My brother Luke was always there for me and could be counted on if I ever needed help which rarely did. Having someone like him to grow and go through things with made me feel like we could take on the world. I have learned about money and happiness my friends. You're close, loved family is worth more than all the money in the world. Money will always be there and you can always just get more of it.

Even at 10 years of age, I remember wanting to own my own business, bad. I remember hearing the legend of how Bruno Contracting started off with nothing and went on to become huge! I remember thinking, "Wow I wish I could do that someday". I still look up to Silvio and Bruno! Silvio has even enjoyed wine with me and answered many questions I asked him he's a very smart and kind visionary man to say the least. I one time did a public speaking opportunity for Shift as a winner of a northern Ontario visionary award at the Airlane Hotel which Silvio had done before me. Humbling that they choose me and two others of the 20 winners to do the talks and my own brother Luke had to buy tickets to hear me speak, even more that several people told me by far I was the best speaker! I discovered something new in myself that day.

Also around this same age, I was bit bad by the weightlifting bug. Part of my life's path was carried in the door by my stepfather Art. He bought a Joe Weider universal weight machine. To my amazement, at 10 years of age, I was able to bench press 160 pounds. Later at school, I found out that this was more than most kids up to five grades ahead of me could do. I spotted a talent in myself.

My brother Luke and I loved guys like Arnold, Bruce Lee and Stallone and we thought that it would be the coolest to be pumped up and manly like them. Sometimes our friends teased us, calling us Hans and Franz from Saturday night live after comedy characters Arnold played, as in "we are here to pump you up". Maybe we loved weight lifting so much because it was one part of our lives that was under our own control. And at that age, you just felt better and more confident every time we surpassed a previous personal best. Talk about a win, win. All this enthusiasm resulted in Luke and I converting the bedroom we shared into a gym. At 10 years of age I was playing around, at 13 I got serious and by 15, weight lifting was arguably the best and most developed part of my life. To me, it was fun, rewarding and predictable. At that age you literally get stronger every week, with every workout. The believing I could achieve something if I tried began with strength training and later in my life the POWER OF BELIEVING proved very valuable.

I was naturally good at any sport I tried. In almost every grade, in every year, I was the fastest sprinter, the highest jumper and the longest jumper. I was a show off though. One time at Whitefish Valley School, I called a teacher over to watch my record long jump for track. At a full sprint, I did a front flip and destroyed the old long jump record. My huge smile got wiped off my face when the teacher said, "Doesn't count. No flips allowed."

A year later I had a chance to go into town for gymnastics. Being so light and strong, I found gymnastics easy. One day they tested us to see how good our skills were. I could already do front flips and could easily do a two-minute handstand, but I had never seen the rings before. With no training on the rings I was able to hold an iron cross. That's when you hold your arms out straight from your sides and all your body weight is held up by the strength of your arms and shoulders. The coaches took my mum aside and told her they wanted to start training me for the Olympics. They explained how at the beginning competition level you could expect to pay over $5,000 a year for coaching, plus travel expenses. By the time you were competing nationally, you'd be paying up to $50,000 a year for coaching. It's so sad that there is little financial support provided for the training of our Canadian athletes. The time required and the cost, were unrealistic for our family, so that was the end of that. I did walk away feeling a little bit special because of my extraordinary skills and now it is a fond memory. I didn't hold it against my mum, as she was working full time and trying her best. Even before becoming a teenager, I could do 70+ chin-ups and 100+ push-ups. Whenever I did things like holding an L shape while balanced on my fingertips and then pulling my legs through my arms and press up into a handstand, it just felt right and beneficial somehow. Growing up a bit poor gave me a hunger to build and acquire wealth. That's why 2/3 of all of the world's billionaires started off broke and worked their way up from nothing. My younger step sisters, Electra and Erica Skaarup did go further in gymnastics and as young girls were winning provincial championships in Calgary.

Weight lifting and strength training may not be for everyone. We all have our own talents and abilities. I had a good group of friends growing up. Some of my closest friends were, Birch Kantola, Dana Donaldson, Matt Scarrow, Trevor and Cory Edwards, Jesse Macdougall, Shawn Potter, Chris Lyons, Chris and James Kaukenen, John Hendrickson, Jesse Hansen and my brother, Luke and cousin, Dave Earl. The weight lifting bug had not bitten them. There must be something written in our Danish Viking and Scottish DNA that has "lift weights" written in. My friends were better at things like snowboarding, hockey, video games and much more. From the ages of 10 -17 my friends would always be excited to show me off. They introduce me to new people by saying, "This is Dan. You have to see his arms. They're unbelievable!" Then I'd show them the peak. This routine went on for so long that my arm muscles got more defined just from all this flexing.

Little did I know that the energy and discipline I poured into my workouts, would be exactly what I would later need to succeed in business.

Many times as a youth, I went off the path and landed in hot water. I was pretty much looking for trouble and excitement. I still hadn't processed the emotional scars I carried from losing my dad at a very young age, due to divorce. My parents are both great people, but they just weren't suited for each other. As a kid you can't understand this, so you carry the hurt deep in your heart. I was blessed to have my step father Art and my Uncle Thorcuill, who tried to fill the gap. Looking back, I can see that I was emotionally charged to grow up, get strong, and get the show on the road. I was in a rush to live.

My Uncle Thorcuill Macdonald had one child, his daughter Emma, whom he loved and cherished. But when he needed some manly time, he turned his attention to my cousin Dave, Luke and me and thank goodness he did. We would box with him until we finally won. Oh, I remember that day! It was like the day that us kids became men. Luke was around 10 or 11. He was boxing Thorcuill and "pow" Luke nailed him on the nose, making it bleed. This sent him running into the house. We were over the top happy when Grandma Rose laughed at him and said, "They finally got you, eh?" Thorcuill didn't let that stop him from pouring gold into our hearts. He would bring us to Scouts where he was our Scout Master. Thorcuill had been a Queen Scout. He literally taught us to "do a good deed every day". He'd play floor hockey with us and taught us how to fold the flag. Sadly, He passed away of a brain tumor well before his time was up. His generosity and influence have lived on in all of us.

My mum had a secret way of motivating us while also empowering us. When all our friends started getting trampolines we begged her to buy us one too. She told us that she would pay half of whatever it was that we wanted and that we'd have to pay for the other half by ourselves. With three of us kids saving our birthday money, saving our allowances and doing whatever other work, like splitting firewood for cash from Arthur, we could save up the $250.00 we needed in a few months. This not only taught us the value of money, but it also taught us pride of ownership. We felt that we had bought that trampoline with our own money. It taught us that we could achieve anything through our own hard work and effort put in.

We were a rough bunch and proud of it. My grade 6 teacher at Whitefish Mr. V told me that he didn't know which way I was going to go. He told me once that the trouble with fighting was that there was always going to be someone tougher than you. He meant well, but I have never lost a fight. Neither has my brother Luke. Adults give kids a dose of cruelty at times that is unwarranted. I clearly remember two neighbors that didn't like Luke's growing confidence. They said, "Just wait until you get into high school. They are going to beat the crap out of you every day." Glad that never happened. Luke went on to become Ontario's Strongest Man, holding the title for 2 years. But the truth is, I don't want to hurt anyone. I worry more for another's safety, than my own. I think it was just our way of holding our own in a world bigger than us.

As young people, we were desperate to pit ourselves against the world awaiting us and become something. I moved out with Luke when I was 15, I had $200 and a belief that I could do it no matter what. Together we got ourselves an apartment beside Churchill high school and the beer store. We felt we were ready to start living life on our terms. My dad Dale gave us $200.00 each month that he paid as child support until 18. Somehow having the rent partially covered helped boost my confidence. I believed I could earn enough to take care of myself. You'd think that all a teenager would have done was party and drink and ditch school, but we were both driven to learn, work, earn and succeed. Sure there was a bit of partying on the side, but first we took care of our responsibilities.

At around 10 years of age I worked as a carpenter's helper. My best friend, Birch Kantola and I worked for Birch's father, Kenny. Later when I was 15, I was paid $8.00 an hour to helped my mum and Art build their new house. So I knew what hard work was. Always had. Since I was going to high school during the day, I knew I needed an evening job. My brother already had a job at Moxies, a restaurant in Intercity Mall, and he helped me get a job there too. I loved my co-workers, but hated being a cook. I was like a fish out of water. My talents were not well suited to cooking. Something just felt wrong, even though the job was actually ok. I worked very, very hard for a year at minimum wage and finally summoned the courage to ask for a raise. The 15 cents an hour raise they gave me felt like a slap on the face with a leaded glove. I'd have to work another 100 to 200 years to see the piles of money I wanted to earn.

And then it happened. I was helping a girl find a job through YES Employment, a youth employment center. There on the job board, staring me right in the face was a job offer wanting a carpenter's apprentice. I ripped off the little paper slip with the phone number on it and called Tangent Stairs MFG. My intuition told me everything was right about this and to just go and do it. I went for the interview with my resume and did my best to get hired. They called me back telling me I'm gotten the job and that I was by far the best person that had applied. At 17, I'd found my life's path. The funny part about that was that I had my heart set on becoming a personal trainer. Carpentry was to be the backup plan.

The only catch was that I had to quit school early and start working full time. My plan was to work days and then complete my high school by correspondence. I finally finished all my credits but it took much longer that I thought it would. Who wants to do school work all evening after working for 10 hours?

Dive in and learn to swim well, that was my style. My carpentry apprenticeship turned me into a man, and young. At Tangent we built spiral staircases, curved staircases, some of them looked like the kind you would see in the movies. Our work would range between a basic set of stairs up to $60,000.00 hardwood masterpieces. My two bosses joked that I had begun my apprenticeship in reverse by starting with the most complex carpentry around.

At Tangent, we had contracts in both Canada and the United States. Sometimes we'd be down in the states for weeks living in hotels and installing staircases. Other times they'd send me down to deliver stairs to Duluth and area. I remember one time when I was around 18 or 19. I started working at 7 a.m. and at 1:30 a.m. I was still driving on my way home. I had to slap myself in the face to stay awake. That's the kind of worker I was, even while getting paid only $7.00 an hour. I helped make these companies piles of money. But I didn't care, I still thought of it as a win, win situation. I traded my time and talents to gain more knowledge. When I first started building stairs a basic set would take me 9 hours to make. A year later I was able to complete the same set in less than 1 hour. My boss Sam was amazed. One day he asked me, "How do you do it? That's faster than we have on our own time sheet." My answer was that for every step I took, I did what was mandatory and no more. Not one step was ever misplaced. I still carried my own personal philosophy I'd learnt while weight lifting: always try to beat your old record. INSTEAD OF COMPETING AGAINST OTHER PEOPLE, COMPETE AGAINST YOURSELF.

It was around this time that I got my own apartment on Arthur St. Luke and I loved each other very much, but we were both alpha males to the max. For me to be able to fully express myself, I had to become entirely self-sufficient. It took me about a year for the investor inside of me to realize that I should stop wasting money paying rent and that I should instead buy a place to call home.

At the age of 19 I bought my first house. It cost $59,000 and had a one-bedroom apartment upstairs and 2 bedrooms on the main floor. It even had a white picket fence. Thank goodness for my mum. Rather than trying to talk me out of it, she encouraged me and lined up several houses for me to look at. The house I bought was one of them. The pressure of being a homeowner at 19 taught me how to manage huge money, even when I didn't have very much. I was smart enough to realize there would be property taxes, heating bills, and bills for water, the telephone, plus the mortgage payment...and then of course you still have to eat. Basically it forced me to turn my home into part income property by renting out the upstairs apartment. Failure is a huge part of success! All successful people have failed more than you'd believe, they just got up and tried again. For the first half a year it was a turbulent ride, but I gradually got better and better at handling it all. Before long I was on my way to having my house paid off in 6 years. For years I strove to make double the mortgage payments and at times was able to drop larger lump sum payment on it.

As a carpenter, I find it easier to accumulate equity rather than cash. Being self-employed, banks often treat you like you're worthless. Unless you can build up some equity, the banks don't want to do business with you. Equity can be anything that you own that has some money value in it. A house is equity. Once you have equity, then you have something you can use as collateral and the banks are happy to lend you money. If you default, they take your collateral.

At Tangent Stairs I apprenticed under two journeymen carpenters: Sam Pollari and Pierre Vroom. I am forever grateful for these two men. They opened the door for me and let me into the world of carpentry. They brought out the best in me and under their guidance and instruction my skills became formidable.

My next opportunity came when Bill Vanlenthe hired me on as his apprentice. I made this happen by calling the college and university's apprenticeship office and lining them up to come out to the job site and sign me up. Bill had promised me that he'd sign me up as his apprentice, and thank god he did. Working for Bill absolutely changed my life for the better. Bill did all kinds of projects, and while working with him, I developed a variety of skills that allowed me to become a great builder. We often built everything from scratch...from the foundation on up. Bill would run a crew of between 2 to 8 people. We did everything from building new houses, to building fire halls, township buildings, veterinary clinics, a 24,000 square foot indoor horse-riding arena, and even raising houses and put basements under them. I liked working for Bill so much I worked with him until I was 23 years old. He was not a very big man but he was braver than most. Although it has been years since he passed away, I still think about him.

My Uncle David Posthumus also worked for Bill. He is Art's little brother. David had called Arthur and asked him to ask me if I wanted a job, as Bill was looking to hire someone. David knew a lot about framing and had worked framing houses in Vancouver for over 10 years. I had first worked with David framing Art's house when I was 15 years old.

I excelled at the college part of my apprenticeship. One the first day of math class at Confederation College, Reese Beerthuizen our teacher walks into class and says, "Alright! If any of you guys think your hot shit you can write the final math exam today. If you get over 80 percent, that's your final mark and you don't have to come back to class." All 32 of us men wrote the exam and tried our best to pass. Funny thing was, I was the only guy that made it. I passed with a mark of 94 percent. I guess all that math I'd learned at Tangent had paid off after all. I spent that time in the college gym lifting weights. After 10,000 hours of apprenticeship and many winters spent learning carpentry skills at Confederation College, I wrote my journeyman exams and passed. I was now a certified journeyman carpenter. Having achieved high grades, I am interprovincial certified all across Canada for life. I joke that I'm Daniel James Bond with a license to build lol my license number even has 007 in it.

Time ticked by and then one day in 2005 I came home from work and told my family, "I just quit my job today and I'm going full time into my own business." They were not very impressed as I only had $2,000 saved up and the bills were still going to be coming in. I dreamed of what I could do and the sky seem to be the limit. We wrote all our ideas down in dollar store notebooks. We were as passionate as we were hungry. I would take every job that came my way. The first few jobs were in the $200 range. I didn't mind. As long as I could feed my family, I was happy. Originally my goal was to make $30,000 a year. Survive first, thrive later, I thought. It was a simple plan that worked and before long my momentum began to grow. I was landing progressively larger and larger jobs.

Hundreds and hundreds of contracts later, I was renovating offices for H&R Block and North American Palladium. I got a new build for a $700,000 duplex and then a giant mansion for a Doctor. At 26 years of age I renovated a 10,000 square foot 3 story office building by the casino for an international exploration company and I was running a 4 to 5-man crew. It wasn't always easy. I'd get anxiety over things like waiting for permits to come in. Sometimes I felt like a kid in the deep end and I had to learn how to swim before it was too late.

During one very stressful period while waiting for permits I started to build my family home, a 2000 square foot, 2 story house. We put a camper on site and I'd get up at 7 a.m. and start building. I'd keep going until 11 p.m. most days until it was too dark to see. I just did whatever I wanted, when I wanted to. There was no one standing over me and there was no one under me that I'd be responsible for. And I loved it! That was heaven for me! If I didn't have to take on work for other people, and I had enough money to float my own builds. I'd build houses like a kid playing Mine Craft. And I have many times in fact I built half the homes on the street that I live floating the whole thing by the university I joke it's my million-dollar corner. When I was building my own house, every bone in my body was telling me that this is what I wanted to be doing. There is this feeling that you get when you take an idea or a dream and make it reality. That is the feeling I get from building, multiplied by many times. Writing this book gives me that same feeling as I imagine the people it will help now and in the future. I know there will be and are others like me that seek out knowledge and apply it for the purpose of reaching their goals and to become successful.

After building the duplex, I realized that I had just built two houses in five months. All I had to do was do that again but this time for myself. We started doing some contracts again to build up more momentum and ended up building a dream home for a client and it was huge. Even alone I can still build over a million dollars of real estate in a year with my own two hands. After building many, many new houses I became a self-made millionaire before the age of 30. As of writing this I'm in my mid 30s and have built in excess of 8 figures worth of real estate with my own two hands. Not bad for a dumb carpenter eh? I now own and invest in real estate across the city and surrounding area and think of it like a video game. I continue to build because it's my life's path and I love it. My family is the only thing I love more. As I'm writing this I am building a 7 bedroom 3 bath two kitchen mansion with and attached garage. See the YouTube video, super carpenter etc. on my channel Daniel Francis and I have... DanSkaarup#2. I believe we created Thunder Bay's first ever time lapse home build video.

MEMORABLE MOMENTS

1. Being there for my family. Nurturing their progressive development has given my life purpose.

2. I've worked out since I was 10 and love weight lifting. I've won numerous competitions for fun over the last 2 decades. Luke and I are both tough as nails. One of the highlights of this was both Luke and I, being in different weight classes, became Thunder Bay's Strongest Man Champions several different times. When I won in 2011 and 2012 I donated my prize money to Camp Quality, (my good deed for the day). Winning was awesome but winning and donating the money to little kids with cancer felt even better. You can check out the YouTube video if you want to see how tough we really were. At 190 lbs. I have flipped an 1100 lb. giant tire after doing 5 others first in Dryden's strongman contest!

3. The YouTube video I'm in that has the most views is "Bench for the Cure". You had to bench press

225 lbs. as many times as you could. The one with the most reps won. I won! The competition raised funds for Hudson B., a little boy struggling with leukemia. Even though this was just a bench press competition, it went on to become Thunder Bay's most viewed strength training video. 250,000 plus views and I benched 225 for 30 reps.

4. In 2014 Shift, a community promoting organization, held the Northern Ontario Visionary Awards, (NOVA) at the Valhalla Inn. All the people in Northwestern Ontario, under 40 years of age, were eligible to be nominated: hence the name The Top 20 under 40. They had 72 nominees, ranging from doctors, to lawyers, to power plant managers. I was so honored to win one of the awards. I think I was the first and only carpenter to have ever won. Apparently not many of the other candidates had created a multimillion-dollar company from scratch. It was rarer than I even realized.

5. To help raise funds for the Regional Health Sciences Center, we sponsored an event for $5000 to be the title sponsor being put on by our friend Sharla Brown of Key Note Events. Paul Lafrance, a famous TV personality from Toronto, was the featured guest speaker. He'd made his fortune designing and building amazing decks and outdoor spaces. Paul builds decks on a lot of Mike Holmes's projects. He even built Mike's own deck. After the event I made friends with Paul and his wife. We were to build a huge deck next to Lake Superior for one of our customers, Mel Pervais. We had hoped

Paul would design it for us. Unfortunately, due to scheduling problems this didn't work out.

6. We took it upon ourselves to design the deck ourselves. The result was the nicest 1800 square foot deck I have ever seen. The design included a bridge, 10 different levels of decks cascading down to the waterfront, 10 staircases, including a fan shaped staircase and a hand carved Thunder Eagle railing. There was a granite bar built around a birch tree, a fire table, a sauna, a hot tub with a waterfall and a waterproof stereo system. This project allowed me to express my stair building and finishing talents to their highest degree. I think even Paul would have been impressed.

7. Since I became journeyman carpenter, I have had a few apprentices work for me. Devon Tucker was one that stood out. He has a heart of gold. We worked together for many years. I was taking on riskier and progressively larger projects. Everyone thinks it would be great to be their own boss but sometimes it just means that you get paid last, only after everyone else has been taken care of. I tried to convince Devon to get paid on the back end of the build like I did. He needed a more regular paycheck than this and we mutually parted ways on good terms. Fast forward a few years and Devon drops by a new home I was building in the Parkdale subdivision. He told me that he was doing great now. He was still being carpenter and had joined the Union. He was making good money, had a girlfriend and had bought a house.

He was even renting part of it out to keep the bills down, just like I had done when starting out. Then Devon tells me, "My life is going so good now and a lot of it is because of you Dan!" Just to hear Devon so strong and happy was one of my proudest moments as a carpenter. I suppose training an apprentice is like lighting one candle with another one.

DAN'S INTRODUCTION TO HIS BROTHER, LUKE

A+ for effort. Mentally tough.

I'd yell "I'm the Ultimate Warrior" and Luke would yell, "I'm Hulk Hogan", and we'd just go at it and we loved it. We could instinctively feel that it was speeding our progress and increasing our toughness.

I've seen my brother; Luke try so hard that several times he went unconscious. Many people are too lazy to even try. This guy is the opposite. As little kids, we would wrestle all the time. We grew up on a steady diet of Schwarzenegger, Rambo and WWE. Our shared bedroom was also our gym. I'd literally climb over the bench press every day to get out of bed. Luke always had an age and size advantage over me. He was usually 80 -100 lbs. bigger and also taller than me. Lots of times me and a friend would go against Luke, just to even out the odds. There were times that we would take it too far and my friend would step aside and watch us go at it in an all-out brawl. One time I got Luke in a double submission lock: an arm bar combined with a leg scissor that was choking him. He would not tap out.

The guy struggled to get out until he went limp and started shaking. I should have let him out ahead of time but I was scared of what he was going to do to me when he did get out. He came to and forgot what had happened. He wasn't even going to kill me. Later I was a little scared of what I had done to my only brother, I mean I love Luke more than I can put into words. A side benefit of going at it with Luke was that no one was ever able to beat me up. They never even came close to his level.

Another time Luke was at the OSM flipping a 1000lb tire and pow! It was like he'd got shot with a gun. A 300 lb. man dropped unconscious on the concrete, back first. It was like a giant tree falling. Thankfully I was right there to help him up and he recovered quickly. I truly believe that Luke's mental toughness is what helped him become the first ever man from Thunder Bay to win the Ontario Strongest Man competition, not once but twice. That makes him stronger than 13.6 million other people. He imagined winning. He trained for it and didn't let anything come in his way from accomplishing his goal.

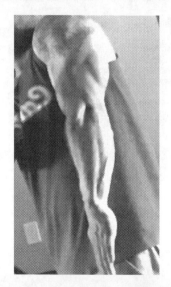

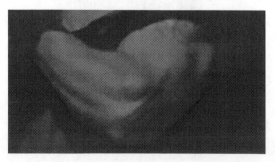

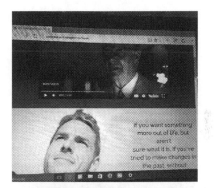

LUKE SKAARUP

(THE IRON VIKING)

Ladies and gentlemen let's get ready to rumble in the jungle! It's time to introduce the toughest man to hail from north western Ontario…. my big brother Luke Skaarup.

In the light of inspiring youth to work out and learning how to gain size and strength I'm going to focus on his athleticism. First off we grew up on part of my grandfather Murry's 400-acre farm. We treated everything as a competition always trying to break our old records. Hay is progressive overload in real life. Luke has always been larger and he decided to start lifting weight seriously as a youth than extremely serious as a man. He would train 3 hours a day six days a week doing the same full body workout!

In high school at Churchill Luke was 265 lbs. in his teens and the toughest guy in our school of roughly 1000 kids and many looked at him as a leader. The nature of working out was very comforting to him because he became more confident, fit, strong and felt a sense of accomplishment. Some people look at exercise as a chore we viewed it as a rewarding hobby that made us feel great.

Strongman begins... his first competition was Ontario's strongest. He placed 9th out of 13.6 million. Leading him to believe that he had a great future. He had never even trained some of the events like the others had. He then decided that he would win and he would do whatever it takes.

Weight lifting is all about progressive overload and making gains. Luke converted his gym into a strongman type gym by buying and building the implements he needed to train to gain strength and win. For example, to have a huge log press you have to have access to a log, train with it every week and make gains on it, if you needed to train it he did! His workouts were extreme, to say the least. I did many with him, he'd train for over three hours at a time, even running with 1000 lbs. on his back up and down the driveway.

All this enthusiasm and hard work paid off as later I would watch Luke on TSN on TV at Canada's strongest man, North America's strongest man etc. he became on fire winning dozens of completions across Canada and the United States. He won Thunder Bays strongest man 5 times Ontario's strongest man 2 times, got 8th at the Arnold classic and placed 4th at Canada's strongest man to name a few. He even set the Canadian record at Dubreuilville for the heaviest atlas stone loaded on to a platform 454lbs. Check out his Wikipedia page or YouTube video's! Out of 60 competitions he reached the podium 37 times and placed first 20 times.... Not bad for an O'Connor lad! He credits his wife Nikki for supporting him and cheering him on.

DAN SKAARUP: SUCCESS PHILOSOPHY MESSAGES

GOALS

Goals are so important. You have to decide what you want imagine the outcome you desire and have the attitude that you're going to get there no matter what. Bruce Lee did this Arnold, Jesus, Nikola Tesla, Bob Proctor, Me, Napolian Hill, Andrew Carnegie most Olympic gold medalists and on and on and on. I am flat out asking you to please add your name to the list! You can be great beyond your wildest dreams don't be scared your spirit can't be killed and your body isn't permanent anyways. My ancestor William Wallace wanted us to know EVERY MAN DIES NOT EVERY MAN REALLY LIVES! Our intention, imagination and faith are supremely powerful things. So much so that many wise men and women from around the world throughout the ages have believed that intention can create form from the unformed substance of the universe. Tesla said that the unformed substance of the universe or dark matter is matter in its alternate state of waiting to take form. Adding electrons to protons creates new elements and on and on the sun gives us life nucularly by transforming one type of matter to another by electrons being added to or taken from electron shells.So add some energy to the substance of all and create a new form or state. Our brain and minds send thoughts out in the form of electrical energy at hundreds of thousands of miles per hour. When you travel you have a destination that you are going to arrive at. Columbus wasn't just going anywhere he decided and set a goal to find the new world. Granted the Vikings found it first but he got many of us to north America. My Dutch ancestors the Estabrooks came here lived near Boston and went to Harvard thanks to him. What did they do after attending and learning at Harvard? Spread the light to mankind to ease its burdens. This is what a goal is. How can you expect to arrive somewhere without first choosing your goal or destination? When you set a goal it activates the creative force of your mind. The more specific and clear your goals are the likelier you are to get there.

Let's say I intend to set a new goal of bench pressing 400 lbs. at a 180 lb. bodyweight (a goal I had and achieved as a youth). First thing my mind starts processing is what am I going to have to do to get there. Activated minds imagine the how. I'd visualize myself getting a little stronger every week and I'd realize that I'd probably have to add in some new exercises because what I'm currently doing isn't enough. Most importantly, I'd get down there and goddamn do it. I'd do my workouts with the intention of getting there, and if you have to turn the dial up a bit more, fine bring it on. Define your goals clearly. Write them down! Better still there is magic in this, write your goals down as already achieved and read them as affirmations daily to pass them from your conscious mind to your subconscious mind! Do this my friend and you're doing magical things to improve your life. I have compulsively and happily studied the subconscious mind since I was 13 years old and I still do that's one reason I love Bob Proctor so much I believe he's the smartest man alive on this topic and he shed extra light for me on a few unlit areas I had. You know the truth when you hear it. It resonates. the subconscious stores 60 000 memories and pieces of information a second, since before you were born. All that has ever been and ever will be it knows of. Edgar Cacey the sleeping profit tapped the subconscious or universal mind to heal people like Jesus and did answer any question in the world they dared to ask him. It is connected to God and the universal and all-knowing mind. It breathes every breath you take and will guide every move you'll need to make to achieve your goals, circulates your blood shows you dreams, beats your heart never forgetting to. You count on it every second to keep you alive and healthy. Why than be scared to count on it to know what to do to reach your goals? I think you should learn understand and apply its forces to get you closer to and achieving your goals. All you need to be successful in life is a worthy goal that you are progressive realizing. No wonder I always felt successful working out since 10 it was that to a tee! The subconscious mind is how the miracles come it speaks to you. Do you know how to hear it? Intuition hunches dreams and more. Affirmation of positive statements and goal will re program your subconscious mind to be more aligned for success. By saying statements thousands of times it does get reprogrammed to give you the outcome you desire. That's why you have to imagine the outcome you desire to teach it the vibration it needs to operate at to make it happen for you. Remember how I said all is energy well all atoms have electron shells giving matter harness to the touch of man or beast. Electron shells are so strange they can take on high and low energy states. All mater is made of atoms and those atoms have electron shells same as our body. And our mind our thoughts, images and brainwaves produce electrical activity that can and does affect other electrons. Study sub atomic particles for many hours and nights as I have and you will come away convinced there is a god 100 percent and God has a mind that thinks and far more. We're talking quarks, muons, gluons, electrons, protons and neutrons etc. they are building and have built those giant colliders to smash matter together like breaking a piggy bank to study the broken pieces. Mankind is blind to much of what goes on and we have very much to learn and understand about the universe still. Magic is possible like sunlight travels at duh the speed of light lol. Well at the speed of light time doesn't exist so a light photon can travel millions of light years and get to earth instantly faster than a second as it feels to it there is no time. The instant it shines the instant it arrives. Furthermore, when it gets to earth it has a mind and thinks as all does. My step father Arthur taught me of experiments where light has been proven to choose if it turns as it goes through a hole. Light decides to turn like us in our truck or car. Wallace D wattles taught us that the universe is alive and it thinks. Just as we do. It's been surmised that spirit sends us thoughts that pass through our mind. All greats of the past have tapped the universal mind like William Shakespeare. When he wrote it's as if god moved the pen in his hand with works of literary genius for him. You become a conduit for the universal mind. Singers I believe do this too, when they write their hit songs that stand the test of time they tap the universal mind. Macklemore raps this in a song "God wrote the song the pen was in my hand I'm just a flawed man". Nikola Tesla I consider to be the smartest man to ever live aside from Jesus himself tapped the universal mind to give us AC electricity the remote control, the electric motor, light up the world starting with Niagara Falls, wireless electricity, florescent light bulbs and hundreds of other things to ease mankind's suffering understood this clearly. Loud and clear Nikola used this to help us all we are blessed and literally energized because of his understanding. He knew how to light up and power the world for free with unlimited electricity via the ionosphere. Felling skeptical? Good so was I look these things up and see the truth for yourself I had to see much of this repetitively from multiple sources across time and the world to become a convinced believer. My imagination is now pumping out huge amounts of electric energy for you and many zillions of atoms will take form in books now and in the future from this energy. See atoms on YouTube they are like tiny magnets glued together made of 99.99 percent hollow space. He even partnered with J.P. Morgan one of the world's richest men and copied the great pyramids foundation designs to build this for us. In case you haven't learned it elsewhere I am happy to teach you that the pyramids were giant energy generators and Tesla knew this and understood how. He respected this power and used it for all our own good. He was 500-1000 years ahead of his time. Why are we humans retarded sometimes, ignorance? Like when a wise man taught us the world was round not flat and we live on a giant ball. We humans went "burn him at the stake" not thanks can you teach us how and why please kind sir. Some of us were sure if you lived on the side or the bottom you'd fall off. That is how we react to new odd ideas sometimes. They hired the army to blow up Nikola Tesla's free energy machine and really took some wind out of his sales intentionally in the process. I love Nikola such a wise man! He was so proud of what he was doing he had them make a time lapse video of its construction. I have seen the video. To grasp the power of the subconscious mind and the power held in imagination please watch Nikola Tesla's You Tube interview, hidden for 116 years! I studied Jesus again as an adult not in a religious context but as a thought vibratory context. Scoping his mindset and attitude just as a wise man and carpenter as I am one myself. He would say "where did you doubt"? he who hath to him shall be given…. the law of attraction in action. Whatever you ask for in prayer believing you'll receive it and you shall receive it. We humans again got jealous and instead of burn him at the stake we nailed him to it in cross formation. Oh the irony of a carpenter being nailed to wood! He used to be the nailer not the nailie. Don't believe in him well what year is it? From when and who? Yep Jesus had a wider influence than anyone you can name. he lives on as the most influential human ever even though he was born in a barn was a carpenter the son of a carpenter and had no formal education. Put religion aside and hear what he was telling you. He had a firm grasp on the hidden forces and powers of the universe. There have since been more than 5 billion copies of the bible printed to tell us of him and others encountering these hidden forces. I'm here alive now telling you to please o please use these hidden forces for reaching your goals. Dare to dream and be the best version of you possible in so doing you'll improve your kids' lives your spouse, family and friends maybe even further like how the McKellar brothers donated a hospital I was born at for free than me loving they're spirit and tenacity writing them into this book to share them with you. Even Oprah the billionaire says that her life's mission that brings the billions to her is spreading enlightenment and understanding to the world. I'm here working at night on the weekend beside my son shining light your way. If you gain even some extra wind in your sales and a little bit of a brighter view of what's really going on here I'll consider this a success.

Reach some smaller easier goals, to get on a roll. There is a lot to be said for understanding how to build up your own confidence. Get yourself on a goal roll and your brain will rewire itself a little more to succeed even better the next time. Celebrating past goals that you have already reached will help you when you need inspiration for taking on your new goals. Goals that can seriously harm you or even kill you should be avoided. Think of Evil Knievel. Everyone knows that guy's goals risked his life. What a stressful existence. When you go all in trying to achieve your goals you'll be surprised at how far you'll go. Think like you do in a game of chess, always thinking several moves ahead. Some goals are hollow. Kind of like when you got an Easter bunny as a kid you thought was solid chocolate than had a tad of a letdown to see it was hollow inside. When you get there it's good but not as good as you had expected. Therefore, decide to go for goals that have some depth on a spiritual level that when you get there you'll feel proud.

We all seem to know about karma. I wonder how many of us know of its cousin Dharma. It's a fancy word for your life's purpose or path. It's what were you sent here to do. OH shit, you didn't know that you were sent here to do something? Well fuck, you actually were... If this is a big news or flash red alert for you, then good. Someone had to break it to you. The happy thing here is that once you are on your life's path, you will be blessed with many good things. If your life has always been a horrible mess and in a disastrous state, then you are likely off the path, and the further off the path you are, the worse things will appear. Conversely, if you have a fulfilling happy life, then you are likely on the path. Goals that are in line with your dharma and your family life will bring you the most fulfillment when you reach them. Hidden in a staircase is the secret on how to reach your goals. You must always take one step at a time, focusing only on make the next step successfully. And you can always somehow make that one step even if the entire flight seems to be beyond your present skills. Or you can try to take 7 steps at once, and trip downwards. That's up to you.

What makes you happy that the more you do it the better your life improves? What are your five best skills and talents that you have discovered so far? What hobbies do you have where you just lose track of time? What would you do if money was no issue? If you really let your mind free what would your goals and dreams be if a genie in a bottle gave you three wishes'? What urges do you have that differ from family and friends, like say do you read or play sports or cook by far the most? These questions should help you find your dharma, if you still haven't. Do your best to make your goals fun and exciting to you. That way you are far more likely to achieve them. If you like me have a goal and dream to start your own business do what my grandpa Aage Skaarup advised me to. Work at another business like the kind you'd like to own one day, learn to run that business and what it really is than go out on your own and you'll know what you'll really have to do. I did exactly that and it worked I've been in business now over 13 years and I am a young man still.

Set your goals with karma in mind. By setting your goals in ways that help others you are definitely heading towards the path. You don't want to have to struggle against the whole universe after all. You ever flip out and the madder you get the worse things go for you until you can feel it? It's like you can feel the karma effecting you. It's like there is a slow car right in my way for Christ's sake and now there's a red light, SOB, and if you keep getting mad then, are you kidding me, where in the hell did this 20-minute train come from. The more you struggle the worse it gets. It's like quick sand. Well let's reverse the flow to the positive. When your goals help other people in win-win situations, everything you touch will turn to gold. Win by giving what you seek.

TALENT

Follow your heart and progressively develop your talents. The five things that your best at, are your respective talents. As you age and try new things, you'll discover new talents. It seems to pay off when you develop your best talents to the highest degree possible. For example, if you are Eric Staal, it makes sense that hockey is your main and most valuable talent. If Eric had quit hockey to play pool or to pursue some other lesser talent, then his life would have ended up drastically different, to say the least. As a good pool player he might have earned $20,000 a year, who knows. But that is a far cry from the $9,250,000 salary he earned in 2015!!! Proving my point clearly. Eric's life may still have been good, but he chose to go all the way for great. That's what I'm advising you to do too. I am a talented carpenter and investor. My talent in carpentry has brought me further than I ever imagined was possible. What helped me to succeed at my goal to become very wealthy before the age of 30? By standing on the shoulders of giants. By learning how others before me managed to succeed, helped to grow my confidence. It grew and grew and yours will too. After all, if they can do you, then you already know that it is possible. By mentally resonating with these thinkers of the past and present, you gain greater understanding, knowledge and motivation to try. Your new found vision and your improving talents will help you advance in your profession at an early age.

When you love what you are doing you'll feel happier doing that. In the end you'll shine brighter because of the extra passion that you put in. The love for what you do will also help you hang in there during trying times, making sure that you get through to the great times. Imagine the outcome you desire and work towards it by using and developing your talents to create whatever it is you want.

GIANT VISION

Call me crazy, but we are one giant human family, with only one race: the human race. When I imagine kids in the future, both yours and mine, I feel great love for them and want the best for them. I've achieved my goals 100 times over and now aim towards helping others improve their lives. There is such a positive effect from learning from the giants of the past. If you put the work in and research and study the past giants, follow the silver thread of your own talents. Then work your ass off trying to build onto what you've learned. Here is a simple example. Bruce Lee is one of my giants that I liked to follow. As a youth my learning was devoted to strength and muscularity. By studying my giant Bruce Lee, I learned that university studies confirmed that the fastest way to increase muscle strength was by doing isometrics almost daily. Isometrics are when your body pushes of pulls against an immovable object for 10-30 seconds. I applied this in my weight training for years and became the best bench presser in the city. No one has been able to beat me for the last decade. My bench press peaked out at an easy 476 lbs., at a 205 lbs. bodyweight. I think those isometrics did help a bit. There is a you tube video called "Bench for the Cure" if you care to see me in action. Some of my friends have joked, "If it's not on tape, it didn't happen."

One time they asked Albert Einstein, "How does it feel to be the smartest man in the world?" He replied, "I don't know. You'll have to ask Nikola Tesla." Albert and Nikola are perfect examples of giants that could be your mentors. These two men weren't perfect, but they both developed the power of super giant vision. Learn from them and you'll come to know that all of their major breakthroughs were first created in their imagination. For Tesla, that's over 700 inventions. Without Tesla's giant vision we would still all be in the dark. I give Nikola Tesla the highest rank of all great thinkers. I have studied hundreds of giants and for me, Tesla is king of them all. He could see things that made him appear crazy to normal folk. And he is there waiting to teach you. There is a YouTube video that was hidden for 116 years, mainly because the world can't handle the truth. Can you? He will clearly tell you how you have a spirit and all things living are connected to you. He teaches you how to nourish your mind and how to create anything using your imagination. When a genius like Tesla comes along, mankind needs to protect, nurture and aid these rare few. But Tesla was horribly abused by his partners and his competitors. He was sabotaged around every corner and many of his ideas were ripped off and used by others for fame and fortune. In the end, his life's work and his business was burned to the ground. But even though he had to endure such maltreatment, he still managed to give mankind things like the remote control, the electric motor, florescent light bulbs and all the motor components needed to electrify the world. Who knows what wondrous works Nikola Tesla could have created if he had been surrounded by people who would have protected him and helped him achieve. Tesla could see how to electrify the whole world and provide us all with free power. But the greedy money people didn't like his ideas because it meant they would not be able to monopolize the distribution of power and Tesla's idea would have prevented them making their huge profits. That's when they decided it was time to shut him down. One day a genius will come along and figure out how to use our sun as a giant battery charger. I believe that god intends us to use our sun as a clean source of fuel and that it will be able to power everything from technology to transportation and provide for all our power needs. Who knows what future geniuses will come along.

REALITY CHECK ON SABATOGE

All right princess, not everyone in the world is your true friend. When the going gets tough, true character shines through. As my friend Ken Boshcoff accurately put it, "You've got your back stabber and you've got your front stabber." Oh man, could Ken be anymore right? Most people prefer to stab you in the back because then you don't know who did it or even know when the knife got there. Keep a close eye on people who manipulate everyone. Chances are, if you watch them cheat on their spouse and routinely lie to everyone else, you'd be kidding yourself if you think that they won't do that to you too whenever it suits them. As you succeed many people will hate you for it. Thank goodness there are others that will cheer you along and be happy for your progress. The best way to compete is to compete against your own personal bests. In this way, you can improve and you don't have to wish destruction on your competitors. If you've done the best you could do, then that's a win in any book. You can still improve and still make friends with this mentality. As you become more successful, you have to increasingly guard yourself. Watch for the ones in your life that tell you one thing and then do the opposite. The truth is seen rather than heard from these types of characters. Your kindness and compassion can get turned into a weakness in the wrong kind of company. As an example, living on part of a 400-acre farm for the first 15 years of my life, we never locked our doors on either our house or on our cars. The first week living in town, we started locking the car because my brother's car stereo and CDs got stolen. I know we were exceedingly naïve but we all get fooled sometimes. I have personally been conned for six figures and it hurts quite a bit more than losing your i phone. One time someone drove a truck through my shop and stole over $20,000 worth of tools, and then they tried to burn it to the ground. Thank goodness the fire never took. My main giant, Nikola Tesla wasn't so lucky. They did manage to burn his livelihood and business to the ground, much to his dismay. There are unfortunately too many people out there that are lower than a snake's arse.

Now for the front stabbers, these are the people who will look you in the eye and smile, all the while screwing you over, seemingly with no guilt, no shame, just pure toxicity. They are so unhappy with their own self-destroyed life that they get pleasure out of destroying other people's lives. Make no mistake, Karma won't forget about them, but they can still bring you down for fun first IF YOU LET THEM I SUGGEST YOU RUN FIRST. These people can be very hard to spot and often they already have your trust. The sad reality is that you have to cut your losses with their kind. The only way to win here is to make them irrelevant to your life. I have tried very hard to keep us on a positive frequency but be forewarned, you'll probably be sabotaged on your way along the path, so trust, but verify. When you have true friends that's all you really need, a few friends not a thousand "friendenemies".

Have you ever heard of the crab bucket analogy? Say you get rich or become successful or whatever, it's like you have climbed out of the bucket. Well some crabs out there will be grabbing your leg trying to rip you down again. They then try to haul themselves up, using you as a living ladder of sorts. Further still, some bastards will even aim to use you as a canoe if they can get you down that far. **In the life and death, action packed battle of crabs, this very book you are reading is a ladder of paper, words and ideas that I and many others have used on the epic climb out of the crab bucket. If we can do it, then so can you.**

On the flip side, you will find people who have a heart of gold and they will always be loyal and true to you. These people are rare and valuable. Do not take them for granted because you will only meet so many of them. If you build a team of fake hollow people around yourself, you will notice that things will begin to unravel instead of growing together. You have to choose your friends wisely. Look more at what someone does, than at what they say. If the two don't match up as true, then you know they cannot be trusted. Life is much more enjoyable and fun, without any knives in your back after all.

PERFECTION

Now let me make this clear. No one is or ever will be, perfect. We all have our own weak area and that's perfectly human. To develop your talents, you do not have to be perfect. You just have to be the best you can be. Chris Farley is a great example. He was one of SNL's funniest guys. Chris had severe drug and alcohol problems and it eventually took his life at a young age. But he didn't let his problems stop him from becoming one of the funniest comedians on earth. In a way, he lives on in his movies. Look at the rock stars or at people like Tiger Woods. Tiger may be highly talented at golf but we all know he isn't perfect. Even when you become a great success in some areas of your life, you'll still have weaknesses in other areas. When you get rich, life does get better, but it still won't be perfect. Your truck can still break down on your way to your grandfather's funeral. People important to you can still pass away. You're going to have to dance in the rain sometimes. Be ready for it. You have to learn to play the cards that life has dealt you to the best of your ability. We are all holding different cards, so we each have to play a little differently also.

WEALTH AND RICHES

Build up your material wealth by understanding and investing in assets. ALSO BUILD MATERIAL WEALTH WITH MULTIPLE SOURCES OF INCOME. Assets put money in your pocket. I have learned a great deal from Warren Buffet. He is so smart it's ridiculous and he presents his ideas in such a true and simple way. When he gets you to follow one of his thoughts on money, you get a feeling like I know this is true. It just makes so much sense. Warren introduced me to the idea of compounding money. Thankfully I read this at a young age. You need to wrap your brain around that concept if you want to build wealth and riches. Compounding money is how you can end up earning more money, and more money, and more money. It's like a giant snowball that grows and grows and grows.

The more money you make, the more assets you buy and the more money you can then make off of your assets.

Start small, start young and start early. The earlier you start investing; the more money your investments can generate. The great news is that you already have a huge asset, your future potential earning. If you work from the ages of 25 to 65 and earn an average of $50,000 a year, you will have earned $2.25 million dollars of income. And that's if you stop at $50,000 a year. For me, by the time I was 33 years old I was building $1.2 million in real estate value a year by being a carpenter with my own company. Just keep progressively developing your talents and you never know where you may end up. I'm not going to tell you that it was easy. It was very hard. Many, many, many things went wrong but I persevered and now it's done. I was s D student because I just didn't care about schoolwork. So if I could pull this off, then image what you could do if you were brave enough to try. Remember what Terry Fox wanted us all to know: IT IS MADE POSIBLE ONLY WHEN YOU TRY. Does this not ring the bell of the POWER OF INTENTION. Terry's good idea of fund raising along with his good intention, raised over $650,000,000.00 worldwide and still counting. Ideas live longer than we do. "Boomshakalaka...like a boss" as my son Daniel would say.

CONFIDENCE

All right cupcake, you want to build up your confidence intentionally so the world doesn't tear you down bit by bit accidentally. I want to build up the strength and confidence of people, but you have to do the work. No one else owes it to you. Anyone who knows me will tell you, "That guy is the most confident bastard out there". Build yourself up by taking very good care of yourself. Your health can be fleeting if left unguarded. Gain small victories by achieving small goals. This will get the feeling of being on a roll and this is a great way to boost your confidence. The more you win, the more likely you are to win the next time. Your brain is rewiring itself and makes winning easier each time. SELF-TALK IS EXTREMELY POWERFUL. The same forces that you attract with your thoughts, come into to play when you think in reverse, so be careful what you are telling yourself. Are you telling yourself, "I think I can, I think I can". Or are you instead telling yourself, "I think I can't. I think I can't." Life is a self-fulfilling prophecy. Be careful what you focus on. If you feel yourself slipping, you have to achieve some small victories to rebuild your confidence. Confidence is like a muscle. Certain activities build it up and other activities tear it down. Pay close attention to what builds you up and what tears you down. Even I went from being able to dead lift a 600 lb. car for 12 – 15 reps to one year later barely being able to walk. After my knee surgery I was fine, but for a while there it got so bad, so fast I couldn't believe it. Simple everyday things like walking down a flight of stairs began to add up big time.

Take good care of your body. You only have one. Eat lots of protein, salads, take multivitamins, eat fruit, take protein shakes, be active, and stay strong. The body becomes what you do. Most machines wear out. The more you use them the more broken down they get. The body is a miraculous machine. The more you use it, the stronger and better it becomes. If you give it the Ideal conditions, your body will thrive. Whatever you like to do, do that. If you like yoga or saunas, do that. If you treat your body well, your confidence will follow suit. If you know you are doing things proactively to take good care of yourself, you will feel better about yourself. That's what confidence is, feeling good about yourself. I know that if I take care of myself I will always improve. And it's not just your body that benefits, your mind will also operate at its highest capacity when the afore mentioned things are in place. Treat your body and mind like a highly tuned, well-maintained racecar if you want maximum performance. Simply put, to be at your most confident, strongest best, get lots of exercise and take good care of yourself. This goes a lot further than you think.

The movie *Rocky* is a good example of how someone can build their confidence up. For those who would like to take confidence building to the next level I would suggest you look up the book *The Winner Effect*. It's a neuroscience book that proves scientifically through clinical studies that proves that your brain will rewire itself and become more confident each time you are able to succeed. Even very small victories can give your brain a big boost. I found this to be a very interesting book. There are even some funny little tips in it that have proven that if you wear a red shirt you're more likely to win in sports, 60% versus 40%, than if you wore a blue shirt.

POINTS WORTH PONDERING AND MEDITATION

- MONEY CAN HEAR CALL IT WITH IDEA'S AND DESIRES
- MEDITATE
- ALL KNOWLEDGE IS EVER PRESENT PICK WHAT'S REQUIRED AT THE GIVEN MOMENT AT THE RIGHT MOMENT YOU'LL KNOW
- LEARN BY HEART
- VISUALIZATION, DEVELOP IT AND BE THANKFULL YOU HAVE IT
- GAIN KNOWLEDGE AND UNDERSTANDING THAT MENTAL ENERGY WILL TRANSFORM INTO WHAT YOU WANT
- BE LIGHTHEARTED AND PLAY ON YOUR MISSION TO LIVE LONGER
- SET TIMELINES TO GOALS
- IMAGINATION IS AN ULTRA POWERFUL FORCE
- FOLLOW YOUR MISSION WITH DETERMINATION
- ASK FOR GUIDANCE AND WORK HARD ON YOUR MISSION
- YOU CAN FORCE YOURSELF TO SOLVE A PROBLEM IN YOUR SLEEP
- IMAGINE PICTURES ON THE SCREEN OF YOUR MIND OF THE OUTCOME YOU DESIRE ALREADY YOURS
- WRITE DOWN YOUR GOALS THAN RE READ THEM AS AFFIRMATIONS DAILY AS A SEED YOU ARE PLANTING IN YOUR SUBCONSCIOUS MIND ITS LIKE THE EARTH

AS IN IT WILL GROW THE TYPE OF SEED YOU PLANT

- WE HAVE EARTHLY EYES AND SPIRITUAL EYES...USE BOTH!
- THE UNIVERSE IS ALIVE AND IT THINKS IT IS SPIRIT (THAT IS HOW YOUR MENTAL MIND ENERGY/POWER IS WORKING OR IS GOING TO FOR YOU)
- ENERGY TRANSFORMS
- THOUGHTS AND IMAGINATION ARE ENERGY AND VIBRATIONS
- ALL IS ENERGY
- ALL IS SPIRIT
- ALL IS THINKING
- ALL IN ALL, IS ALL WE ARE
- ALL IS ALL MADE OF ONE SUBSTANCE
- ALL IS ALL CONNECTED
- ALL HAS ALTERNATE STATES JUST AS WATER CAN BE ICE LIFE GIVING LIQUID OR CLOUDS ABOVE
- GIVE VALUE GO ABOVE AND BEYOND
- SET DREAMS AND GOALS FIRST SPIRIT WILL SEND IDEAS THROUGH YOUR MIND AS TO HOW YOU'LL REALISE THEM AFTER
- STAND ON THE SHOULDERS OF GIANTS THAN FURTHER THEIR WORKS
- EVERYTHING IS ENERGY/ELECTRICITY, FIRST LIGHT THAN MATTER AND ELECTRONS TRANSFORM MATTER INTO NEW ELEMENTS
- ATOMS HAVE ELECTRONS AS SHELLS OBITING AT 5 MILLION MILES AN HOUR

- THERE IS MATTER AND NEGATIVE OR DARK MATTER WAITING TO TAKE FORM IT IS FORMLESS UNTIL ENERGY SWIRLS IT TO LIFE AS WE WOULD KNOW IT
- LIGHT SPEED IS 671 MILLION MILES AN HOUR SOME SAY THOUGHT IS FASTER
- ENGAGE IN YOUR CAREER BECOME A STUDENT OF IT
- RADIATE FORGIVNESS, LOVE AND GOOD WILL TO ALL YOU GET WHAT YOU GIVE
- -GIVE GOODNESS
- KNOWLEDGE IS ONLY POWER WHEN YOU USE IT TO ACHIEVE GOALS AND DEFINATE AIMS
- YOUR ATTITUDE DETERMINS YOUR ALTITUDE. WITH A POSATIVE ATTITUDE BEING THANKFULL TO ALL YOU'LL BE SUCCESSFULLY FLYING HIGH
- MEDITATE IN ALPHA MIND STATE 10 HZ/SEC
- BE DECISIVE ITS CRUCIAL
- START OR CONTINUE WITH POSATIVE AFFIRMATIONS
- AFFIRMATIONS REPEATED ARE SEEDS PLANTED IN THE SUBCONSCIOUS MIND
- YOU THERE YES YOU!! YES, YOU CAN DO IT YOU ARE AS GOOD AS ANYONE ALIVE OR DEAD. ALL IN ALL, THIS IS TRUE.YOU CAN BE A GREAT PERSON OR A HAPPY PERSON IN THE HISTORY BOOKS IF YOU DECIDE TO NO MATTTER WHAT
- FAITH COMPOUNDED WITH PERSEVERANCE HAS SUPER POWERS

- PLAN TO SUCCEED DECIDE WHAT YOU DESIRE AND GO AFTER IT, IF YOU FAIL DUST YOUSELF OF AND TRY AGAIN AND AGAIN UNTL YOU SUCCEED LIKE A BABY LEARNING TO WALK
- ALL SUCCESFUL PEOPLE HAVE FAILED MANY TIMES BUT THEY DID NOT QUIT THEY PERSEVERED. MICHAEL JORDAN WAS CUT FROM HIS HIGH SCHOOL BASKETBALL TEAM RATHER THAN QUIT HE PERSEVEERED UNTIL HE WAS THE BEST BASKETBALL PLAYER ON EARTH.
- BE A CREATOR USING YOUR IMAGINATION AS A CREATOR OF THE FUTURE AND YOUR BODY AS A TOOL TO DO THE WORK OF ASSEMBLING YOUR VISION
- LET GO AND LET GOD/ THE UNIVERSE
- LEARN ABOUT THE UNIVERSE, IT'S LAWS AND GOD, THAN SEND ENDLESS APPRICIATION AND LOVE AND THANKS
- IDEA'S WITHOUT ACTION ARE USELESS KNOWNING IS NOT ENOUGH YOU MUST DO THE WORK. YOU MUST APPLY YOUR WISDOM
- BE POSATIVE AND THANKFULL TORAWDS ALL AND MAINTAIN AN ATTITUDE OF GRATTITUDE
- COMPETE AGAINST YOURSELF SETTING PERSOANL RECORDS FOR THE THRILL

YOUTH BUILD UP

Building your way up, from the bottom to the top. I've been there at the bottom, eating Kraft dinner, Mr. noodles and cookie dough, with not much else in the fridge. We're talking about when you are so poor that you are actually hungry borderline starving much of the time. Hungry for money and success but hungry for food too, for Christ's sake! I know how it feels when all you can think of is "What am I going to do?" "How the hell am I going to get through this?" "Where do I start?" I feel for you. I went through that and made it through to the other side and I'm kindly here telling you how to make it.

Rather than focus on the despair of having nothing, focus on working through to the other side. What baby steps can you take now in the right direction? No matter where you want to get to, by taking steps in that direction, no matter how small, WILL START the process of you getting there. Even the greatest journey begins with one step. Say you have a goal, and that goal is now the image of a 7000 step staircase, with the top being where you want to get to. I hope we can all agree that it's a waste of time to try and jump all 7000 steps at once and just end up falling off. But it's perfectly clear that if you just take the first few steps, and then some more steps, and then just keep going at a sustainable pace, you WILL get there. And as you keep taking steps your subconscious mind will become programmed to just do it for you with ease. This is like our lives. Too many people want it all right now but won't take the steps necessary to getting there. It's like they want to be at the top after taking only 12 steps and if they're not then they quit and say that it's impossible. It's someone else's fault and they shouldn't have to put up with this crap. Sadly, I have never found the goal escalator that you just climb on and let it bring you to the top with no effort on your part!!!!

Learn to ask the RIGHT question. Many magical things can happen. A new invention is the answer to a question that hadn't been asked yet. To get you through, questions are the keys that open doorways in the right direction. What do you want out of life? Do you want kids? Do you want to be married? What are your talents? What makes you different? What are you best at? What do you lose track of time doing? What are you most happy doing? What type of business would you like to own? How could you start a small business? What would you name it? What would it do? What kind of business would let you use your talents? How can you make money and still help people? What are your goals on how to get there? Do you have to eat special food? Is there any training that you'll need? Is there a school that will help you grow your talents? Are there groups of people with your same talents that you could learn from? If you could make it rich or famous or do whatever you wanted to do, what would you do? If you could have anything in the world, what would you fill your dream house with? What color would your dream house be? Would you have pets, a garage with toys? Do you have a helicopter or a racecar? Hey it's your dream. You are harnessing the power of visualization. Hey, my grandpa Aage Skaarup built his own ultra-light plane and flew it when he was in his 70's.

I want you to ask 100's of more questions like that and I want you to write them down in a book so YOU KNOW WHAT YOU WANT. Now that's your motivation to get off your ass and take those steps again and again no matter how boring or whatever, you know where it's taking you and you know it's going to be worth it. I routinely have to remind myself at times, why am I doing certain things. Like, why am I putting so much effort into this? Oh yeah, ok, ok, it's going to be worth it in the end if I GET WHAT I WANT. It takes some self-coaching at times. Even if you just want good arms, you're going to have to do many reps and endure many workouts before you start to see any development. People who have made it have known that there is a connection between the work process (steps) and getting the results you want. This is where your focus and discipline come in. You are the one that keeps you on the path to your goal. By focusing on what it is you want, you will be able to draw on extra strength and stamina when you start feeling depleted. It pays off to be self-motivated, to be able to feel your direction deep within. Other people don't really care about your goals and probably don't even know you have any. Again, build your way up there, step by step.

Say your goal is to be your own boss and one day own your own business. One of the first baby steps would be to land some small sales form your friends, relatives and customers even for a dirt cheap price. Like a kid with a lemonade stand, after selling your first glass, you have proven the concept to yourself first. If you don't believe in your business, then no one else will either. If you can't get even tiny sales at reduced prices, then move on to your next business idea. Think of an idea that gives you goose bumps it's so good. Follow the stream of money and grow your business. If you set up a lemonade stand and sold 10 cookies and 1 glass of lemonade, follow the stream of money and increase your cookie selection and increase the amount of cookies you have for sale. Even if you had planned to sell mostly lemonade and maybe a cookie here or there, you've got to be real with yourself and listen to what the market is telling you. Too many people get attached to a particular idea they like but the market doesn't. If you started selling coffee too and ended up selling 50 cups of coffee and still only 1 glass of lemonade, well listen to what the market is telling you. You now are the proud owner of a coffee and cookie stand. I did a $200.00 repair job and breathed life into Skaarup Construction in 2005. Adapting and evolving is the key to business success. This applies to even larger scale dreams. Say I'm a homebuilder and want to sell new homes. If I build two $700,000 homes and no one can afford them or wants to buy them....???, I will have to adapt and start building homes in the $300.000 to $400,000 range. Follow the money stream to grow your business. Help make the world a better place with your business, and it's a win on many levels.

I wish you all great success and happiness in life. The ball really is in your own court. THE WHOLE UNIVERSE IS YOURS TO CREATE WHAT YOU WILL! No one else but you can play the game. Keep your eyes open, your head up, and your heart in the game and I know you, with one step at a time, you will get there when you think and act in a certain way that resonates with your dreams and desires. Improvise, adapt and overcome that's what we all have to do in the quest off success. As of 2-20 seconds from now you can become instantly successful. How I'm hoping you ask? Decide this second to strive to reach a worthy goal your aiming for and promise yourself and me that you are going to get there no matter what!!

With a Steve Jobs level of faith. Like when they threw him out of Apple and he decided to start a company called Pixar! Steve became instantly successful when he decided, defined and committed to the goal. Steve was so smart he had his employee's create the computer mouse out of a butter dish and grocery store supplies! He later sold it to Disney.

Apply what you have learned towards realizing your clear worthy goals and desires with unwavering faith and perseverance! May the rest of your life be the best of your life, love and many good blessings to all.

Stand on the shoulders of giants my friends!!!!!! Do this and I HAVE NO DOUBT that you'll become ultra-successful at what you choose to and BECOME BLESSED BY DESIGN.

MY GIANTS

NIKOLA TESLA
TERRY FOX
WARREN BUFFET
BOB PROCTOR
NAPOLIAN HILL
STEVE JOBS
SANDY GALLAGHER
EARL NIGHTINGAL

ANDREW CARNEGIE
ELON MUSK
WALLACE D WATTLES
BILL GATES
DANIEL
ISAAC NEWTON
BUDDHA
JESUS
ALBERT EINSTEIN
BILL GATES
ARNOLD SCHWARZENEGGER
J.J. CARRICK
THE MCKELLAR BROTHERS
ROBERT KIYOSAKI
STEVE JOBS
EAGAR CACEY
HENRY FORD
NORMAN PATTERSON
WILLIAM WALLACE
BRUCE LEE
NEIL DEGRASSI TYSON
MIKE HOLMES
ALSO MANY MORE

GIANTS AND FREINDS

DALE SKAARUP
MURRAY MACDONALD
BILL VANLENTHE
MEL PERVAIS
KEN BOSHCOFF
ARTHUR MARTIN

CHRISTINA MACDONALD
LUKE SKAARUP
AMBER SKAARUP
KENNY KANTOLA
SILVIO DIGREGORIO
PAUL LAFRANCE
CHRIS SKAARUP
HAL SKAARUP
THORCUILL MACDONALD
WALTER RAY ESTABROOK
AAGE SKAARUP
SAM POLLARI
PIERRE VROOM
DIVID CHILTON
AND MANY MORE

ABOUT THE AUTHOR

Daniel J Skaarup is currently an award winning CEO and founder of a successful home building and real estate development company. He is also a success coach to the mass's having been trained by Bob Proctor an international best selling author (featured in the book The Secret). Daniel is an entrepreneur to the maximum having started his first business at 23 years old and became a self made millionaire before 30 years old. Never one to sit still he is an award winning visionary and now an author himself. He is a very strong man having won many strength championships and loves to exercise and encourage others to become the best versions of themselves. He is a family centered man and father. Daniel has been educated at Confederation Collage in Thunder Bay Ontario four times and is a red seal carpenter holding a perpetual journeymen licence in all provinces of Canada. He has repaired and built over 2000 homes in Canada and the united states. Being an old soul and eternal student of the universe he has a habit of standing on the shoulders of giants that he is now spreading to the world. Daniel is the type of person who radiates love, understanding, forgiveness and good will to all. He now aims to help others across the world maximise their potential after seeing what the right attitude and thinking process's has done for him. He lives in Ontario Canada with his family and friends happily. He perpetually seeks out and absorbs the wisdom of the ages and mentor's instinctively and now most important of all he is here for you! Ladies and gentlemen lets get ready to rumble in the jungle.